God Wants You To G[et The]
Most Out Of Life Before It Gets
The Most Out Of You!

Conquering Life's
Challenges. . .

By Marty Ritzke

Balboa Press books may be ordered through booksellers or by contacting:

Balboa Press
A Division of Hay House
1663 Liberty Drive
Bloomington, IN 47403
www.balboapress.com
1 (877) 407-4847

ISBN: 978-1-9822-2030-3 (sc)
ISBN: 978-1-9822-2031-0 (e)

Library of Congress Control Number: 2019900801

Print information available on the last page.

Balboa Press rev. date: 03/19/2019

BALBOA
PRESS
A DIVISION OF HAY HOUSE

> "No man understands a deep book until he has seen and lived at least part of its contents."
> American Poet Ezra Pound

TABLE OF CONTENTS

Introduction

I started this writing journey many years ago. I've always loved writing poetry and journalism in school. In 1990 I had a frightening bout of metastatic papillary carcinoma. The papillary cancer initially started in the lymph nodes in the neck area. It apparently spread to surrounding areas including the parathyroids and thyroid gland. This is where the surgeons had to do a total thyroidectomy along with removing 48 lymph nodes. There were numerous complications during the surgery. The doctors didn't think I would make it. Apparently that was not true. God had a plan, and it wasn't my time to go. I was coming in and out of the anesthesia and overheard a doctor say: "Oh my God, is she going to make it?" Another doctor answered: "I don't think so, get the _____." I saw something go over my face. It was cold, and most likely pure oxygen.

Right after that I experienced something very unusual. It was an outer body experience. I saw myself on the table, and could tell exactly where doctors and nurses were. I looked at the heart monitor and saw it do a flatline. It wasn't long after that I was back under anesthesia. Hours later I was in the recovery room and my doctor came in and began telling me about the ordeal. He asked how I was feeling, and I couldn't talk. Apparently my left vocal cord was paralyzed and the other wasn't functioning properly. I ended up having to write my thoughts down on paper. I wrote: "Dr. Meglar, you are a pain in the neck!" and handed it to him, then fell back asleep. The next morning he came in and asked if I remembered anything from last night. I didn't and he retold me what all happened. He then showed me what I wrote him. Afterwards, all of us started to laugh.

This is when I began the adventure of writing a book Get The Most Out Of Life Before It Gets The Most Out Of You. I began the lengthy process of reading, researching, and writing on ways people can get the most out of their lives. Diet & nutrition, exercise, the power of prayer, laughter, massage, visualization, communications, even stress and how to minimize it, were topics I wanted to be in the book. My desire was to show people different ways to improve the quality of life. Unfortunately the original copy got lost when my computer crashed. I didn't have a back up like an external hard drive or an additional way of saving it. Without anything but the original documents, I began the tedious task of re-writing the book. As time passed I began venturing out more into the spiritual realm. The idea of 'Spiritual Lessons in Life' took hold and the rest all fell in place.

I have always had a passion for laughter, photography and animals. I love being able to capture them in the moment while reflecting their personalities. All of us can agree there is something special about animals. They are an integral part of our lives. I'm grateful for the many opportunities I've had to capture so many awesome animal photos. Some inner voice, spoke to me. It said: *'why don't you use some of those wonderful even hilarious photos in your writing and get others to enjoy them and even laugh more.'* Well, I loved that idea, and it catapulted into something I think people of all ages will enjoy.

> "None of us got to where we are alone. Whether the assistance we received was obvious or subtle, acknowledging someone's help is a big part of understanding the importance of saying thank you."
> Harvey Mackay

I Give Special Thanks To:

This book, is in dedication to my mother. She was such an inspiration and mentor in my life. Her upbeat positive outlook along with her creativity rubbed off on me. My mothers unconditional love, support and understanding really helped pull me through so many of life's challenges. She was always there for me. No matter what others would say or do, she always saw the good in me and could make it apparent. She would see me through, not through me. Unfortunately she is not here to travel this journey with me, but I believe she is looking down and smiling.

I can also think of so many people to extend a sincere "Thank You" to! I really don't know where to begin. I could actually write another chapter on all of the wonderful people I am grateful for. They have been such an inspiration to me throughout the years.

~ I want to extend a sincere "Thank You" to my family for all of their support. I want to thank my father, Linda and her daughter for their input and support along the way. I especially want to thank my brother Dave. He was such a tremendous mentor. His passion for creative writing along with his knowledge were such an inspiration. His insight, and guidance helped me to achieve this dream while sharing my gifts. He always was a motivating force offering constructive criticism throughout my writing journey. His input helped me to come up with the design I'm currently using in this book. He told me: "Do more with my photography. That is, to let the pictures tell the story." Without his help and guidance, this book wouldn't be like it is.

~ I give special "Thanks" to my husband Gary. His patience and encouragement throughout this venture made such a difference. His input and support is greatly appreciated. Gary bought me the Canon's EOS 7D with the Canon 100 - 400 mm Image Stabilizer lens. Later on he got me the Canon Power Shot SX720 HS, and can zoom from 24-960mm along with the Canon EOS 5D Mark IV. This awesome combination along with patience, persistence and fantastic timing helped me capture the many awesome wildlife photos used in this book.

~ I also give special "Thanks" to my dear friends Joan and Jerry Kruzel and Linda and Tom Pacic and Clint Cavern who continually offered unconditional love, support, encouragement, inspiration and wisdom, along with prayer throughout this endeavor. They sure helped me get down life's bumpy road more easily. Their input and ideas along the way kept me motivated me to write this book. I am deeply grateful for their integrity, sincerity and support throughout the years. They helped me get where I am currently in life.

I Give Special Thanks To:

~ I want to say "Thank you" to the many friends, acquaintances, clients and doctors who all have offered me support along the way. I'm pretty sure you know who you are. I also want to thank the staff and trainers at the Apple stores who have been helpful teaching me ways to creatively design the pages in the book. I also want to extend a sincere "Thanks" to the many authors that have all fed my insatiable appetite to learn. Their shared information and lessons had made a tremendous impact in my life. Some of those awesome authors are Louise Hay, Joel Osteen, Anthony Robbins, Norman Vincent Peale, Zig Ziglar, John Maxwell, Norman Cousins, Bernie Seigel MD, Allen Klein, Dale Carnage, William Clement Stone, Napoleon Hill, Jack Canfield and so many more. I'm grateful for them sharing their knowledge and wonderful information to readers.

~ I also give "Thanks" to The Seaside Seabird Sanctuary located in Indian Shores, Florida for providing me an awesome opportunity to get close to so many wild and tame birds. These birds are doing what comes naturally to them. This provided wonderful opportunities to capture wildlife in the moment in their natural setting. So many of the photos used in this book were taken there, along with other wildlife parks, beaches and places where animals like to hang out.

~ Now they say: "Save The Best for Last." Well, I'm about to do that. I especially want to extend a sincere "Thank You" to our Almighty God for giving me the gift of life, along with the necessary talents and contacts to be able to create and complete <u>Conquering Life's Challenges</u> in the series <u>God Wants You To Get The Most Out Of Life Before It Gets The Most Out Of You!</u> I am working on. Without His blessings and guidance, I don't think this would have turned out the way it did. God provided me opportunities to capture awesome wildlife photos, writing skills, a sense of humor along with inspirations to help me share His word. I certainly am grateful for God's blessings and guidance.

"On the recollection of so many and great favours and blessings, I now, with a high sense of gratitude, presume to offer up my sincere thanks to the Almighty, the Creator and Preserver."
William Bartram

God Gets You Through Troublesome Times!

Photo By Marty Ritzke

"Lots of things happen each day. Lord, thank you for getting me through those troublesome times. I sure can enjoy life more knowing You are there for me!"

"God always gives His best to those who leave the choice with Him."
Missionary Jim Elliot

God Gets You Through Troublesome Times!

All of us at one time or another run into troublesome times. How you handle life's challenges can make a difference in the outcome. So often it's easy to let these challenges become overwhelming and control your destiny. Sometimes you may feel like they're relentless, even out of control, or there is nothing you can do to change what's happening. You can think defeating thoughts, or you can think thoughts like: "I know God will help me get through it." When you give in to those problems you are simply allowing them to get the best of you instead, of getting the best out of them. Understand your reactions can make a difference in the outcome. During those unpleasant, troublesome times try to be aware that God is always looking out for your best interests.

It is worth repeating. No matter how bad those situations may seem, God is looking out for your best interest. He will not let those situations ruin you. He always has a plan. So, please understand as unfortunate and uncomfortable as those situations may seem, they are lessons God uses to strengthen you. God knows your interests and what makes you stronger, so why not let those situations work in your favor. You don't have to control everything. By doing that you are showing God you understand your life is in His hands, and there is no reason to let situations get the best you.

When you release your desire for control, you're giving God the thumbs up to continue with His plan. You're also showing your faith and confidence in Him. By simply "letting go and letting God" take control of your life, you're allowing Him to perform his mystical, magical feats. You also are allowing God to open new doors and close old ones. God only wants what is best for all. He doesn't want anyone to feel discouraged. Instead, He wants us to be encouraged. As Pastor Joel Osteen frequently says in his services: "God wants us to be victors not victims." He wants us to realize our problems are not the end to life's story. They're simply another paragraph in the chapters of our life. God will get you through your challenges. He'll only give you what He knows you can handle. Why not show God you understand that by handling those challenges and be ready, willing and able to conquer whatever is thrown your way.

"Honey, Do You Understand That God Is Looking Out For You?"

"The difficulties of life are intended to make us better ~ Not Bitter!"
Anonymous

God Strengthens Us Through Troubles!

Photo By Marty Ritzke

If it weren't for God's help I'd be going 'nuts' trying to solve all my problems. It's comforting knowing God is there for me!

"Strength does not come from winning. Your struggles develop your strength. When you go through hardships and decide not to surrender, that is strength."
Actor Arnold Schwarzenegger

God Strengthens Us Through Troubles!

Life's many unexpected surprises can be challenging. Maybe it's a phone call from a loved one with unfortunate news, or an accident, or some unpleasant news from your doctor. Sometimes life's surprises can bring you happiness. It could be a letter from an old friend, good news from your doctor, a promotion, or bumping into someone that can help you fulfill your dreams. When these things happen, please know, what may seem surprising to you is simply part of God's plan.

Whether your problems are big or are small, God will bring solutions to them. I love how Mother Theresa believes God only gives us what we can handle. Every time I think about her belief I can't help but smile realizing my life is in God's hands. Nothing can change God's plans. So, with that in mind, I simply keep looking forward knowing God will always bring triumph at the right time. Sometimes it's hard to see it that way. It's easy to get wrapped up in the situation and lose sight of what God is doing in our lives.

When times are tough and situations seem hard to handle, you may want to give up or simply say: "It's not going to work out." "Why should I bother?" That's the easy way out. Instead, why not realize life's tough times are simply lessons God uses to strengthen you. Sometimes during those moments it may be hard to see that. But if you can look at those challenges as lessons, and try to learn from them, you'll find a peaceful calm that prevails. What a difference not getting all stressed out will make in your life.

Those unexpected challenges that pop up become easier to handle when you realize God is in control of everything. It also becomes easier to stay calm and be at peace with what happens. God already knows what's in store in your life even before you do. When you're aware that you'll realize life's occurrences are simply God's plan. John Quincy Adams once said: "Patience and perseverance have a magical effect before which difficulties disappear and obstacles vanish." Since the outcome is in God's hands there's no reason to let things get the best of us. Why not leave those difficulties to God? Let Him help you get through those challenges.

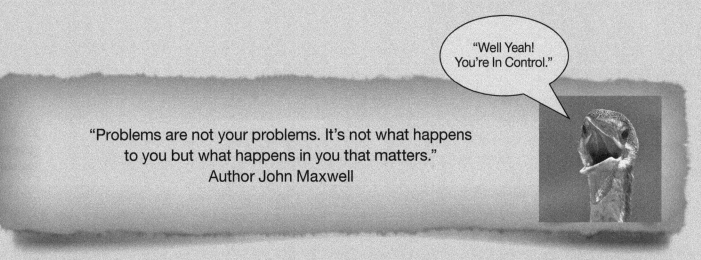

"Well Yeah! You're In Control."

"Problems are not your problems. It's not what happens to you but what happens in you that matters."
Author John Maxwell

Leave It To God!

Photo By Marty Ritzke

Lord, I realize You want my life to be full of joy so I can share it with others.
I want You to know, I'm thankful You keep filling me with hope,
even though I occasionally bark up the wrong tree.

"God will never direct us to be prideful, arrogant and unforgiving, immoral or slothful or full of fear. We step into these things because we are insensitive to the leadership of the Holy Spirit within us."
Senior Pastor Charles Stanley

Leave It To God!

All of us have problems we must get through. That is inevitable. Some are worse than others. One thing that is for certain, God already has solutions before you experience any problems. God knows what He wants for you and will give it on His terms. God has a plan to get you out of your troubles. Whether it be health related, financial, interpersonal, business troubles or even loneliness. They will come to pass. God will provide the necessary strength needed to get through life's many problems. He also will give answers to your questions and solutions to the problems you face. All you have to do is ask!

When asking God for help please know, He will be there guiding you every step of the way. Scriptures often talk about 'call out to God and He will answer,' and to 'ask so you shall receive.' It's important to know, and understand, God won't let anyone experience difficulty without providing help to get through it. God will not get you into something that He can't get you out of. The situation you're currently facing may seem difficult, unattainable even impossible. Your health problems may seem like they're never getting better. Your finances or even your work situation may seem grim, relationships aren't working out as planned, but realize one thing. You need to view these problems as opportunities to see how powerful faith, prayer and God Almighty truly are. Like it says in Job 22:21 NLT, "Submit to God, and you will have peace; then things will go well for you."

All you need to do is keep the faith and continue believing. By staying in faith, God will bring you out better than before with even more happiness. Having faith requires believing something before seeing it. When you stay in faith, you are trusting God, knowing He has a plan for your life. God wants you to get into an agreement with Him, knowing everything has its season. Where you are in life is only temporary. In Corinthians 4:17 NLV it says: "The little troubles we suffer now for a short time are making us ready for the great things God is going to give us forever." Ann Landers also put it so well when she said: "Where we are is temporary, not permanent. Expect trouble as an inevitable part of life. Repeat to yourself, the most comforting words of all; this, too, shall pass." That's great advice to follow. So, give your troubles to God. Let Him find resolution. By doing that you can easily rest in peace and go on living a happier life.

"Really? That's Good To Know."

God Is Comforting!

Photo By Marty Ritzke

Much like God, I'm here for you dear.
Please understand, we unconditionally love you and will always look after your needs.
So don't worry or be afraid. Instead, pray and let us know your concerns.

"I want to challenge you today to get out of your comfort zone.
You have so much incredible potential on the inside.
God has put gifts and talents in you that you probably don't know anything about."
Pastor Joel Osteen

God Is Comforting!

Unfortunately all of us experience challenges in life. How you handle them determines the outcome. Adverse circumstances can get the best of you, or you can learn how to get the best out of them. That choice is yours to make. Pastor Joel Osteen often says in his sermons, "God wants us to be victors, not victims." That is so true! In other words, God wants all of us to be happy, healthy, strong and achieve our dreams. God wants to provide abundant favor and blessings throughout life. God doesn't want you to simply accept where you are currently are in life, or stop trying to live life to its fullest.

You may notice during difficult times there's a need for comfort. According to Webster's Dictionary, comfort means; "to give strength and hope; to ease grief or trouble." Whenever someone offers comfort, they provide assistance and support during tough times. This comfort helps you get through those times of need or grief more easily. Sometimes no-one is there to be supportive and help comfort you. So when you face challenges alone, turn to that which is familiar, reinforcing and soothing. For some people it may be exercise, or their work. Others may find their pets or friends are calming. Even enjoyable activities like watching movies, music, crafts, reading or writing can ease tensions. Certainly you are familiar with eating "comfort foods." It's a natural tendency to want something that is comforting during tough times. Personally I turn to God for comfort. So during stressful times think about what brings you enjoyment and tranquility, and pursue it.

I love what someone once said. "When the going gets tough, the tough get going!" With that in mind, know there are answers to life's uncomfortable situations. Once you realize you can find them, take action. No matter what difficulties you may be facing, God's desire is for you to be strong and confident, while having hope and faith. It's easy to let life's distractions pull your thoughts away from God. You need to trust Him and understand He wants to comfort you. He wants to provide pleasurable feelings of peace and calm, well being, and contentment, especially during uncomfortable times. So, during tough times, simply turn to God and pray. Let God's love empower you and lift you up to higher places while helping you over-come life's many obstacles.

You'll Be Glad You Did That.

"Mommy Makes Me Feel Good, But God Really Comforts Me!"

"God will not permit any troubles to come upon us, unless He has a specific plan by which great blessing can come out of the difficulty."
Pastor Peter Marshall

**"And let us not be weary while doing good, for in due season
we shall reap if we do not lose heart."
Galatians 6:9 NKJV**

Don't Give Up And Quit!

Photo By Marty Ritzke

Lord, I need Your help. It's hard to keep going when times are tough!
Sometimes I just want to call it quits. I don't want to be a quitter,
so I'm asking You to help me not do that!

**"People of mediocre ability sometimes achieve outstanding success because they
don't know when to quit. Most men succeed because they are determined to."
Trial Attorney George Allen, Sr.**

"And let us not be weary while doing good, for in due season we shall reap if we do not lose heart."
Galatians 6:9 NKJV

Don't Give Up And Quit!

Throughout life you'll experience situations that seem to be out of your control. It's easy to let them get the best of you. When this happens, you may want to give up. Sometimes quitting is easier than trying to get through life's challenges. Possibly you've experienced something like this. Believe me, you're not the only one. Quitting may seem like the easy way out, but really, it isn't. So often if you quit you'll be worse off in the long run, as opposed to pushing through life's challenges. I love what Norman Vincent Peale once said: "It's always too early to quit." As you conquer life's challenges, one thing is for certain. Experience is an excellent teacher. It actually strengthens you for upcoming challenges that will inevitably come your way.

As you go through tough times it is tempting to abandon your goals and dreams. Instead of giving up, why not turn over a new page in life. It may be what is needed and part of God's plan. So instead of quitting, why not turn to God, pray, and ask for guidance. Praying sure is better than giving up. God will answer prayers! So be patient and know it will happen when He feels the time is right.

Troublesome situations are inevitable. When they occur, you may not know how to jump over those hurdles. That's okay. When you ask God for help, you're actually letting Him know you are not a quitter. You are showing Him you want to do what it takes to get ahead in life, but simply need His help.

When life's challenges bombard you, and you need to somehow conquer them, remember, it takes determination to not quit. Inspirational author Napoleon Hill put it so well when he said: "You can be anything you want to be, if only you believe with sufficient conviction and act in accordance with your faith; for whatever the mind can conceive and believe, the mind can achieve." It is worth repeating. "What the mind can conceive and believe it can achieve." Keep one thing in mind when going through life's challenges. You can always turn to God. No matter how tempting it is to quit, remember, God can, and will help you conquer life's challenges.

"My Friend, Don't Give Up. OK?"

"Don't quit. Never give up trying to build the world you can see, even if others can't see it. Listen to your drum and your drum only. It's the one that makes the sweetest sound."
Author Simon Sinek

Don't Quit Because of Setbacks!

Photo By Marty Ritzke

Someone told me 'Don't let disappointments upset you … just get on with it.'
Lord, I used to have a hard time getting through disappointments.
Lately, I'd rather turn to You knowing You'll pull me through.

"When you can't control what's happening, challenge yourself to control the
way you respond to what's happening. That's where your power is!"
Unknown

Don't Quit Because of Setbacks!

Undoubtedly you'll experience trials and tribulations. It's tempting to get discouraged when things don't turn out as planned. When it feels like troubles are surrounding you, that's the time to dig your heels in and say, "I can quit, but I won't. I'm not giving up because God gives me strength in times of need!" The good news is, God promises He will make good on those setbacks. In order to get relief, you need to be patient and let God preform His duties. What that doesn't mean is He will immediately relieve you from your burdens. God may not do it on your schedule. So understand, in due time God will confidently give you the strength to get through life's challenges and persevere regardless of the obstacles.

You may agree that nobody goes through life without experiencing some sort of tragedy. Like someone once said: "It's always darkest just before the dawn." Even though challenges are unavoidable, you'll notice sometimes, situations get worse before they get better. Maybe you've noticed, like I have, some of your challenges either go away or become easier to handle. Some may even seem funny? Actor and comedian Steve Allen once said: "Tragedy plus time equals comedy." When I look back at situations where I wanted to quit, I often see comedy in them. So, if you happen to be going through setbacks, remember, life is full of absurdities. Keep pushing through them! Understand those setbacks can actually strengthen you in the long run. Also, have faith and trust in God. Know He will help you get through those tough times.

When going through difficulties or setbacks, understand, they aren't permanent. They come, and they go. When setbacks happen, keep the faith and remember to continue thanking and praising God. Many verses explain how our current troubles are small and won't last long. A great example is from 2 Corinthians, 4:18-NLV where it states: "We do not look at the things that can be seen. We look at the things that cannot be seen. The things that can be seen will come to an end. But the things that cannot be seen will last forever." With that in mind, it is to your advantage to be patient, and keep trying. Also don't give up and quit. Instead, set your hopes higher, stir up your faith, and keep believing in God. When you do, you'll see the victory God has for you!

"I Don't Quit, Instead I Just Keep Trying!"

"Most people who succeed in the face of seemingly impossible conditions are people who simply don't know how to quit."
Pastor & Author Robert H. Schuller

God Helps Us In Times Of Trouble!

Photo By Marty Ritzke

Lord, I realize troublesome times are part of life.
How you handle those situations can make such a difference.
That's why I like giving my troubles to You! I know You can, and will help me.

"Speak to Him often of your business, your plans, your troubles,
your fears - of everything that concerns you."
Italian writer, Alphonsus Liguori

God Helps Us In Times Of Trouble!

Ever notice some people experience tough breaks more often than others? What seems interesting is, somehow they manage to get through them. You might have noticed during tough times it's nice having someone there to help you along the way. Helping others is an act of kindness that can make a difference in their lives. You may have heard of actress Audrey Hepburn. She once said: "Remember, if you ever need a helping hand, you'll find one at the end of your arm. ~ As you grow older, you will discover that you have two hands. One for helping yourself, the other for helping others."

When you help others you are actually shifting your focus from your problems to making someone's life better. During that time, your attention is off yourself. Have you noticed that your problems seem to lighten up and solutions may come more easily when you stop dwelling on them? I sure have. Sometimes I've noticed they even go away. I've also observed when you primarily focus on problems they can become overwhelming, even to the point where solutions are hard to find. I love what Margaret Thatcher once said: "Watch your thoughts, for they become words. Watch your words, for they become actions. Watch your actions, for they become habits. Watch your habits, for they become your character. And watch your character, for it becomes your destiny. What we think, we become." Wow! What you focus on becomes your reality. Like someone once said: "If you think you can - or can't, - you're right."

You truly are what you think, so try not to focus on troubles and complain so much. Instead, shift your focus to more desirable thoughts. One way to do that is to let God simply guide you towards the answers. By giving your concerns to God, allowing Him to take care of them, you may begin feeling more tranquil. You may notice problems are still present, but now they're in your peripheral vision. Zig Ziglar, motivational author and speaker put it so well when he said: "Be grateful for what you have and stop complaining - it bores everybody else, does you no good, and doesn't solve any problems." Realize tough situations are actually lessons you can learn from. Those experiences may make you want answers to questions like: 'What's expected of me?' 'What can I learn from these experiences?' 'Who can I turn to for help and confide with?' These are great questions. I recommend not putting all your attention on questions like that, because it could cause a delay in finding answers. It's okay to wonder why? But, instead, why not tap into God's power? Let Him help you get through those troublesome times you are facing. .

"I Like Talking To God. He Helps Me Through My Problems"

"Problems are not stop signs, they are guidelines."
Pastor & Author Robert H. Schuller

Believe God And Earnestly Seek Him!

Photo By Marty Ritzke

Dear God, please know I believe in You!
I turn to You and ask for guidance whenever it's needed.
I know You're always there for me, and I want to thank You!

"Before we can know God and understand His great plan it is first necessary for us to believe that He exists and that He rewards all who diligently seek Him."
Judge Joseph Franklin Rutherford

Believe God And Earnestly Seek Him!

Challenges and obstacles are simply unavoidable. You might have gone through, or are currently experiencing some. So often when going through setbacks it's easy to think about what you don't have, might lose, or have already lost. Unfortunately thoughts like these amplify negative feelings and can have an undesirable impact on the outcome. During difficult times one thing is for certain. You always have the freedom of choice! Now that is a beautiful thing. You can either focus on what isn't working out, letting discouraging, negative thoughts affect the outcome, or you can shift your focus to more positive thoughts. Like I've said before, another choice is to simply 'let go and let God' help you through those challenges.

It's recommended not to waste time on negative thoughts or what you don't have. Instead, focus more on being grateful for what you already have. Look for what is positive in the situations you face each day, instead of the negatives. If you are stuck in traffic, why not enjoy some music you like, or listen to something educational instead of getting all frustrated? Oftentimes people think, 'I'll feel better when I get healthier, or I get a job, spouse, or out of debt.' 'I'll thank God once I get through these problems.' Understand, faith doesn't work that way. As long as you are negative, discouraged and keep focusing on your problems, it limits what God will do. Why not start utilizing the time God gives you each day being more grateful? In advance why not thank God daily for the blessings He's going to give you? Even though you don't know what they are, you still can start each day with thoughts of gratitude and praise like 'Thank you Lord for another day filled with your blessings.' When you do that, it'll open doors for God's blessings.

Start praising God to spite what's going on. Thank Him for another beautiful day. When you do that, you shift your focus to more pleasant thoughts. Positive changes definitely start happening. Windows of opportunity will open. You'll experience situations that make you think, 'Wow! Did I hear you right, You're going to give me____? How amazing!' 'Or I just met someone who____.' 'I don't know why I stopped here but I ran into___ and they're going to help me get ____.' Meeting the right people at the right time will occur. Maybe you've experienced something like that. You might have even wondered how could that happen? One thing is for sure. You need to think big. Ask God for favor that is above and beyond your expectations. By doing that, you'll notice God rewarding you. Without any doubt you'll find peace and happiness once you believe and earnestly seek Him.

"Lord, I Believe In You And Know You're Here For Me."

"Everything comes to us that belongs to us if we create the capacity to receive it."
Author Rabindranath Tagore

Trust In The Lord!

Photo By Marty Ritzke

God only wants what is best for everyone.
My friend, why not let Him help you get the best out of life?
I'm telling you, it's worth the effort!

"I give all the glory to God. It's kind of a win-win situation.
The glory goes up to Him and the blessings fall down on me."
Olympian Gymnast Gabby Douglas

Trust In The Lord!

Trust is all about having a firm belief in someone. I'm sure you'll agree. All of us want, deserve and need to be trusted. Good relationships are built on trust. Trust is something you have to earn. Honesty and sincerity definitely play a part in developing trust. Winning someone's trust requires acting in ways that are trustworthy. Being responsible, dependable, honorable, reliable, loyal and faithful are a few ways you earn someone's trust.

God also wants you to have trust in Him. God inevitably will provide when your actions show you trust Him. When you trust God, He will offer guidance in unimaginable ways. American Olympian sprinter Allyson Felix put it so well when she said: "I have learned to trust God in every circumstance. Lots of times as we go through different trials, following God's plan seems like it doesn't make any sense at all. God is always in control and He will never leave us." That is so true. God's plans may not be the same as ours. The timing of His plans may be different too. Realize, if you have faith and trust in the Lord, He will come to your aid when He feels the timing is right. God will always fulfill your needs and answer your prayers.

With that in mind, you can see how so many scriptures talk about the power of faith and trust. One that comes to mind is Romans 8:31 WEB. "What then shall we say about these things? If God is for us, who can be against us?" The message so many scriptures tell us is to trust God and know He will take care of your needs. You just have to let Him. All too often we try being the almighty conquerer tackling our problems without turning to God for help. Have you done that? If so, did you notice you got all stressed out and frustrated if not overburdened, especially if it doesn't work out as planned? During those overwhelming moments you should turn your challenges over to God. Ask Him for guidance and know you can get answers. When you show your trust in God, He will begin to bless you with His favor.

By acknowledging God in all you do, giving Him thanks and praise, He will direct you in ways that are hard to imagine. Pastor Joel Osteen put it so well when he said: "God can cause opportunity to find you. He has unexpected blessings where you suddenly meet the right person, or suddenly your health improves, or maybe you're able to pay off your house. That's God shifting things in your favor." God's plan is for all of us to be happy, healthy, prosperous and live in peace. So let's have trust in God and believe He will lead you down the path He intended you to go down.

"I've Seen What God Has Done And Will Continue Trusting Him!"

"All I have seen teaches me to trust the creator for all I have not seen."
Ralph Waldo Emerson

Praise God For What He Does In Your Life!

Photo By Marty Ritzke

Lord, You've made such a difference in my life.
That's why I'm giving You all the praise You deserve.
My life would be so different if I didn't trust and believe in You.

"Develop an attitude of gratitude, and give thanks for everything that happens to you,
knowing that every step forward is a step toward achieving something bigger
and better than your current situation."
Motivational Speaker, and Author Brian Tracy

Praise God For What He Does In Your Life!

Each and every day there are so many opportunities to give thanks. It can be something as simple as thanking someone when they open a door for you, or compliments you. What about thanking a cashier for prompt service, or a family member, or someone special for simply being a friend? I bet you have a few people you are thankful having in your life. I sure do. When we're together I like finding ways to show my appreciation, and give thanks whenever possible, knowing those words will go a long way.

The simple act of saying: 'thank you' can have such a positive impact on people. Those few words carry a lot of weight. Have you ever done something nice for someone and never got a 'thank you?' How did you feel when they didn't acknowledge your act of kindness? I bet you were a bit annoyed, if not put out. I can't blame anyone for feeling that way. It's true, a simple 'thank you' gesture could have made you feel differently. Those few words don't take much to say, but sure can go a long way with others.

To spite what goes on in your life, look for what you can be thankful for. Understand God hears everything you say and responds accordingly. Sometimes it seems impractical giving thanks to unpleasant situations. For instance, you weren't able to get to your destiny in a timely manner. By arriving late, you missed something you wanted. It's easy to think, 'Why should I be thankful for this?' Later you find what you originally wanted wasn't as good as you thought, or you may have missed a serious accident due to the delay. Those delays may have simply set you up for something better. Like in Psalm 68:19 NLV it says: "Honor and thanks be to the Lord, Who carries our heavy loads day by day. He is the God Who saves us."

When you praise God for all He does, you not only make Him happy, you feel good too. You're showing Him your gratitude and acknowledge His power. In return God offers abundant favor. So praise God for what goes on throughout your day, like the food you're about to eat, getting a break in the traffic, timing the lights or even a phone call you've been waiting for. It's a great habit to get into. Believe me, He hears you. These little acts of appreciation go a long way with God. He will continue giving you blessings, both big and small. God will close doors that shouldn't stay open and open doors that you may not have known were there or couldn't open yourself. So throughout each day give thanks to God, not only for what He does, but also what He doesn't do in your life. You'll be glad you did that.

"I Always Like Giving Thanks To God!"

"Since His delights are to be with you,
let yours be found in Him."
Catholic Bishop Alphonsus Liguori

God Works Behind The Scenes!

Photo By Marty Ritzke

Lord, I want to thank you for creating my life to be everything it is.
You work behind the scenes helping me fight battles, catch fish, and guide to victory.

"God wants His people to be the most blessed! He wants His people to increase so
they can live as an example of His goodness. But in order to partake of everything
He has in store for us, we have to be open to what He wants to do in our lives."
Pastor Joel Osteen

God Works Behind The Scenes!

I've said it before and I'll say it again. No matter what happens in life, one thing is certain. God constantly works behind the scenes helping you move towards your destiny. Sometimes it doesn't seem like it, but God always looks out for your best interest. Maybe you've been praying about something and nothing seems to be changing. You might be going through some hardship. Maybe you've have experienced something like that. It's natural to get angry, upset and frustrated when things don't turn out as planned. But, that is not what God wants. God wants His people to be blessed and live happy productive lives. When you're doubtful, apathetic and negative, you are showing God you don't trust Him. When this occurs, God simply backs down and waits to give His blessings. So shake off disappointments and negativity.

God wants you to believe and put your trust in Him. By trusting God, you're showing Him you accept and understand He has a plan for your life. When you must tolerate life's difficulties, put your trust in God. When you know something better is on the way, He will start giving His blessings. Pastor Joel Osteen often talks about difficult times and how they strengthen us. "Have you ever noticed that it is in difficult times that we grow stronger? That's when we are being stretched. That's when God is developing our character and preparing us for better things." Even though it is for your improvement, many people may not like 'being stretched.' Often it puts a strain on you causing uncomfortable feelings to surface. Please understand, that is a normal way to feel.

Interestingly enough our thoughts dictate what happens in life. In Proverbs KJV 23:7 it even says: "For as he thinketh in his heart, so is he..." When difficult times don't ease up, or prayers aren't answered right away, please know, God listens and hears every word you say. He knows what's best and will continue providing ways so you can fulfill your dreams and passions. He wants you to receive every blessing that's in store, so you can live a life filled with happiness, love, and His favor. To spite what's happening, God doesn't want you to be weary, lethargic, apathetic, doubtful or negative. He doesn't want you to sit back not trying to do your best. Understand God knows exactly where you are. Trust God, knowing no matter what you may think, He is constantly working behind the scenes. He determines your destiny and makes no mistakes.

"God Fulfills My Needs. Like Food, Water, & Friends!"

"If God can work through me, He can work through anyone."
Saint Francis of Assisi

God Has The Pieces To Our Life's Puzzle!

Photo By Marty Ritzke

God, I need Your help. I want to put the pieces to my life's puzzle together.
I can't seem to find them all. I used to think something was wrong.
Now I realize it's part of Your plan.

"God has the pieces to the puzzle of your life. Because it is incomplete that puzzle may
not make sense right now. Don't get discouraged. There is another piece coming."
Pastor Joel Osteen

God Has The Pieces To Our Life's Puzzle!

You may have heard the analogy that our life is like a big puzzle. When the pieces to this puzzle come together, they show our many facets. The challenge is putting it all together to tell our story. At times certain pieces are hard to find. Initially it's hard to know where all the puzzle pieces are, or where they will go. Sometimes you may not even know where to start looking. Other times, you may not see the picture as a whole. At times it's easy to get wrapped up in your life. You work hard at accomplishing things, while not getting the desired results. Maybe you've wondered what to do, or had thoughts like; 'I've been praying about ____, will I ever get results?' 'What should I do?' 'What's next?' or 'What's expected of me?' I've had thoughts like that, and it's understandable.

Sometimes missing pieces are in places that are unpredictable or where you may not think to look. Like the puzzle, the same holds true in life. When this happens, you simply need to step away, and come back to it at a later time. By doing that you may see things from a new perspective. One thing is for certain, God knows exactly where the pieces are and where they go in our lives. Sometimes it seems overwhelming, but to God, it is easy. He knows your needs and will guide you, if you let Him. Many times you act according to your thoughts, doing what you think is right. Sometimes it's not always what God wants you to do. So understand, where you want to be may not be where God wants you to be.

Life's many uncertainties are like that unfinished jigsaw puzzle. You'll notice putting life's pieces together gets easier once you accept God's plan and can be at peace with yourself. Ever notice sometimes the pieces don't look like they'll connect? Occasionally what you are looking for is right in front of you. Maybe you need to see it from a different angle. When pieces don't seem to fit, all it takes is finding one, then it gets easier putting a few more together. Like in life, you may need to make a few changes so things can come together more easily. At the time it may not seem relevant, but in the long run those changes can make a difference. One significant change you can make is to turn to God and follow His Word. If you are having trouble doing that, understand, God can get results. He knows what's best for everyone. When you notice God has your life planned, you can mentally step back and let Him perform His miracles. So believe in God, and understand He has the pieces to your life's puzzle all planned and will help you put it all together.

"I Guess I'll Wait
And See What'll
Be Next."

God Has A Plan And Purpose!

Photo By Marty Ritzke

Lord, I know my life is in Your hands. I don't want bad things to happen.
Please help me fight those battles that come my way.
Keep me safe and under Your protection.

God Has A Plan And Purpose!

As you've learned, God has a plan and a purpose for everything in our lives? It kind of makes you wonder, doesn't it? I certainly think about that. God's plan may be unknown, but one thing is definite. God designed us to live life to its fullest. God gives each of us special gifts and talents to pursue. He already knows what you need and what you'll be doing. God provides the right opportunities to come your way. He also sends people to help you when needed. You might have noticed some people want to control everything in their life. At times, this can be more of a hindrance than it is helpful. They think they can handle situations and get answers by themselves and try to change things that only God can alter.

A better option is to peacefully center your thoughts on the fact that it is God's will, not ours, that determines what'll happen in life. Sometimes it seems like God isn't answering our prayers or changing the situation we are in. Like many of us, you may have experienced something like that. There may be a good reason why. It should be easier handling life's events when you recognize God knows your needs and will find answers at the right time. Every so often timing doesn't seem right, but it's worth mentioning again. What happens in life are lessons God uses to teach and strengthen you. So keep an open mind and learn from those valuable lessons. Sometimes situations are hard to understand. Please grasp this fact ... God constantly works behind the scenes improving your life. He doesn't just want you to go through challenges, He wants you to grow from them.

Hopefully you can realize God doesn't want you to be anxious, sad, upset or even angry. God wants you to be at peace with what He's doing. He wants you to know your life is in His hands. God's desire is for you to live happily and with love, while be comfortable where you currently are in life. He wants you to believe He's going to fight your battles. So trust God, because no matter what you may think, He is constantly working behind the scenes. In Exodus 14:14 NKJV it states: "The Lord will fight for you, and you shall hold your peace." Those who understand that can handle challenging situations more calmly and easily. Once you turn your challenges over to God and realize your battles are in His hands, those problems, both big and small, become easier to handle. You'll begin seeing God's blessings come your way. My advice to you is, have faith and understand God has a plan in your life.

"Lord, I May Not Know Your Plan, But I Bet It's A Good One!"

"As your faith is strengthened you will find there is no longer the need to have a sense of control, that things will flow as they will, and that you will flow with them, to your great delight and benefit."
Dr. Emmanuel Teney

God Only Dishes Out What You Can Handle!

Photo By Marty Ritzke

Hey it's true! — I've gone through a lot and still have trust in God.
He helps me get through life's challenges.
Sometimes I'm not sure why, But it always works out.

"God chooses what we go through; we choose how we go through it."
Author John Maxwell

God Only Dishes Out What You Can Handle!

No matter what God's plan is, unpleasant situations undoubtably occur, even unexpectedly. No doubt you have experienced some yourself. When that happens, it's easy to think: 'I'm going through so many hardships. I don't know if I can get through them.' 'I'm not sure what can be done about this.' As you experience challenges, realize, they're simply lessons from God. Those lessons actually make us better. They're intended to give you the strength to handle what is yet to come. I love the quote from Mother Theresa which is on the pillow. It's true, God only lets us go through situations He knows we can handle. They are lessons from God. They may seem annoying, troublesome, even distressing. They might even be challenging, but understand, our reactions can truly make a difference.

Difficult times are inevitable and unavoidable. One thing is evident! When they occur you can choose how you react during those uncomfortable situations by accepting what happens in life. Remember, decisions directly impact the results you experience. Situations can control you, or you can take control over them. They can either be overwhelming or a learning experience. You can give in or even give up, or you can decide to let God help guide you through those troubles. Why not think of those experiences as lessons from God, and you are the student. A friend once shared a quote by Lao T'zu that is so true. "When the student is ready to learn, the teacher will appear." Anytime we are ready to tackle something new, or try to accomplish something, it's to our advantage to let God guide us through it. Our reactions to situations can have an enormous affect on the result, and ultimately our lives.

Since troubles are inescapable, when they happen, remember God has a plan. He only gives you what He knows you can handle. Joel Osteen once said: "God doesn't want you to change the situation, but to have the situation change you. To spite your troubles know that God has a good life in store for you. Keep looking ahead as you continue learning and venturing forward in life." Understand God wants triumph to follow you wherever you go. God already knows what is best for all of us. He simply wants you to achieve your dreams and improve the quality of your life. He also wants you to share your gifts and help people along the way. God put in each one of us exactly what is needed to live a good life. So to spite some of the negative situations you may be going through, realize they're going to make you stronger and improve your life. They were not meant to pull you down. So keep the faith and let God preform his miracles throughout your life. You may like the outcome. .

"You Know, That's Really True!"

Faith . . . It's A Must Have!

Photo By Marty Ritzke

Lord, I'm not sure what's going to happen today, but I have faith in You.
I believe in You knowing You'll bring me good things.
Maybe it's people to play with,
go on walks with or even give me treats.

"I am only one, but I am one. I cannot do everything, but I can do
something. And that which I can do, by the grace of God, I will do."
American Evangelist Dwight L. Moody

Faith . . . It's A Must Have!

Faith is what moves God, allowing Him to be an integral part of your life. When you have faith, you are making room for God's favor and blessings. When you put your trust in Him you'll find an abundant increase in God's favor. Maybe you had something happen where the timing was just right. You got a call from someone you were just thinking about or you've prayed for something and it was answered at the right time. Well, God's timing is different than yours. He times things in your life in such a way that the right people are at the right place at the right time. He will continue putting opportunities in front of you. God wants to do mysterious and magical things that will improve your life. Realize those blessings are His way of appreciating your faith and trust.

You'll find it gets easier to comfortably take more chances throughout life when you venture out in faith. Unfortunately, some people don't tap into this power. Life throws challenges that seem hard to handle. It's easy to get caught up in the moment. You may have even experienced something like that. Challenging situations demand your attention and dominate your time. If you let that happen they can actually take control of your life. You may even start losing your faith. When that happens, your faith remains blurred and stays in your peripheral vision. You may realize faith exists, but if it's not your main focus, you may lose sight of God's blessings and limit what He will do in your life.

Maybe you've wondered will things turn out as planned. You may have had thoughts like: 'Will I ever get out of debt?' 'Will I get a raise or a promotion at my job?' 'Will I ever get married and have a family?' 'Can I get past my health challenges and live a happy, healthy life?' That's perfectly natural to think thoughts like that. The fact is, all of us have faith. Faith can help you get through life's many challenges. Everyone has the ability to utilize this power to better their lives. Once you realize that, and act accordingly, it becomes easier to grasp God's amazing powers. You'll begin to notice faith is something we must have. It's worth practicing and can become an integral part of your life. Initially it may seem hard to do, but like anything, the more you do it, the easier it becomes.

So keep the faith. It truly is a great habit.

"Faith Is A Must Have, Without It I'd Be Lost."

"Basically there are two paths you can walk: faith or fear. It's impossible to simultaneously trust God and not trust God."
Pastor Charles Stanley

Faith Is Something We Need!

Photo By Marty Ritzke

When I got into an agreement with God, my faith really grew.
He showed me faith gets results. Since I put my trust and faith in God,
He rewards me with so much favor.

"Believe in yourself! Have faith in your abilities! Without a humble but reasonable
confidence in your own powers you cannot be successful or happy."
Author Norman Vincent Peale

> **"But without faith it is impossible to please Him, for he who comes to God must believe that He exists and that He is, and He is a rewarder of those who diligently seek Him."**
> **Hebrews 11:6 NKJV**

Faith Is Something We Need!

Life isn't always fair. It relentlessly throws unpleasant experiences your way. Life's many disappointments can pull you down. No doubt you've gone through tough times. When going through difficult times you really need to tap into your faith. When you experienced setbacks, did you tap into your faith to help you get through them? Or, did you think: 'things just don't seem to be working out for me?' Please understand, all of us are blessed with faith. It allows you to put your fears, frustrations and negative thoughts to rest as you take a quantum leap into the unknown. Saint Augustine once said: "Faith is to believe what you do not see; the reward of this faith is to see what you believe." That may be hard to comprehend, but the truth is, everyone has the ability to use this awesome power of faith.

In order to live a blessed life, it's important to have faith and grasp hold of its powers. Franklin D. Roosevelt put it so well when he once said: "Let us move forward with strong and active faith." Unfortunately, some people don't regularly tap into this power. They wonder about God and whether having faith will get them through their troubles. It's true, when you don't have faith it can limit what God will do in your life. When you don't put faith into action or you stop thinking about it, you're actually allowing it to stay in your peripheral vision. It becomes easy to forget about. It reminds me of that wonderful saying, "Out of sight, out of mind." Realize with faith, you make room for God's favor and blessings. So be bold in your belief. Have faith and confidence in God Almighty.

Faith and trust work hand in hand. One guaranteed way to put faith into action is to diligently seek God. Praise and worship all that He does, to spite life's unfair turn of events. So step out in faith and live by God's Word. When you do that, you are motivating God to bless you. God will award those who honor Him and live according to His Word. No doubt positive changes will occur when you take that leap of faith. Nothing gives God more joy than when you step out in faith, and show your trust in Him. This trust removes any limitations you may have so God can begin preforming His miracles in your life. Let Him go to work for you. Keep letting faith be your guide. When you do this, you'll start noticing God doing supernatural things in your life. His favor will come your way in abundance. So call on the Lord and hear His answers.

"I Trust and Have Faith In Everything You Do!"

"I think faith is incredibly important because you will become overwhelmed with what's happening and you will have waves of grief, but when you turn to your faith, I believe God will give you waves of grace to get through it."
Pastor Joel Osteen

Call On Me, And I'll Answer!

Photo By Marty Ritzke

Dear God, I understand desperate times call for desperate measures.
So I will call on You to help guide me through life's tough times.
I know You'll answer me in times of need.

"Call to me, and I will answer you, and will show you great
things, and difficult, which you don't know."
Jeremiah 33:3 WEB

Call On Me, And I'll Answer!

Inevitably during hard times people turn to God wanting to trust Him for answers. They pray hoping their problems get solved. Like many, you may have even done that too. You pray while wondering will He answer them. Well, God wants you to know, He hears you, and will answer your prayers according to His plan. Please understand, God's ways are different from your ways. Nothing happens randomly. Everything has a purpose. The timing may be different or not be in agreement with your plans. What's important is to realize everything is part of God's plan. He knows what is in your best interest, even though it may not currently seem like it. He also knows the ideal way for you to achieve His plan. Once you're aware of that, it becomes easier practicing patience and being happy where you are in life.

The situations you face today are no surprise to God. They are simply part of His awesome plan. God knows the results even before they occur. That's hard to imagine, but it's true. He already established your end before the beginning. We shouldn't let life's challenges get the best of us. Instead we should get the best out of them and simply call on God. Author Mary Manin Morrissey, wrote: "Have you ever struggled to find work or love, only to find them after you have given up? This is the paradox of letting go. Let go, in order to achieve. Letting go is God's law." As you start doing this, practice thinking thoughts like: 'God thank you for doing what only You can do.' 'Lord, I'm thanking you in advance for answering my prayer(s).' I say this prayer whenever I am in a vehicle. 'Lord, thank you for getting me to my destiny both safely and effectively. Please safely guide me as you protect my car and all cars surrounding me, for I am in the palm of your hand. If there are any complications along the way thank you for not letting anything bad happen on the way.' These kind of prayers will make God happy. Be cognizant that God will answer your prayers when He feels the time is right.

When you understand, God works behind the scenes and hears your prayers it becomes easier to live with a more tranquil attitude. By showing your faith and trust in Him, you're encouraging God to give you His blessings all throughout the day. You'll see it gets easier to call on the Lord, knowing He will answer your prayers in His time and in ways that are magnificent. Joel Osteen often says: "Problems may seem big, but God is bigger. If God is before you, who dare be against you?" Now that's a great way to look at life's challenges. Why not live each day with the attitude of gratitude, knowing all things are possible when you believe in your Almighty God? Why not call on Him in times of need and let Him guide you through life?

"It's True, God Sure Helped Me Out In Times Of Need!"

"Do all things without grumbling. Why? You have a sovereign God who is on your side, who works everything together for your good."
Pastor John Piper

God Looks Out For Our Best Interest!

Photo By Marty Ritzke

Lord, I appreciate how You always look out for me.
I understand my best interest may not be Yours. So, whatever happens,
I know You'll lead me to what's best in life.

"Never be afraid to trust an unknown future to a known God."
Author Corrie Ten Boom

God Looks Out For Your Best Interest!

Many people ask: 'What's in my best interest?' It is common to want you know what would be best for you. Ever notice, sometimes it seems like you are either running to or away from something? You may even wonder if there's anything you can do about it. Well, you're not the only one experiencing something like that. Granted, plans don't always turn out as desired. When that happens, realize God is constantly looking out for your interests. Sometimes it doesn't appear that way. You may have experienced troublesome times that seem overwhelming with no resolution. When going through something like that, it's easy to think: 'It's too hard to handle.' 'I can't deal with this,' or 'It's not going to work out.' But thoughts like this only hinder God's desire to help you work though those tough times.

One thing is for certain, problems are inevitable. Some more challenging than others. Life's trials and tribulations must be dealt with. Please know, how you handle them will affect the outcome. You can do your best to avoid them or be in a state of denial, thinking: 'If I ignore it, maybe it'll go away.' 'Possibly in time it won't be so bad.' Another option is to face problems head on and do your best to conquer them. Believe you will get through them successfully. It's good to know when facing problems head-on, God is testing your faith. He wants you to trust Him and to understand He's always looking out for your best interest.

God has a plan for your life. He already has solutions to your problems even before you experience them. It gets easier conquering life's challenges once you know and believe God always looks out for your best interest. As your trust grows, along with your faith, you'll notice you may even start taking unpleasant situations in stride. Those challenges are lessons we can learn from. So take charge. Open God's floodgates and allow blessings to come your way. As you face life's challenges, remember to focus on the wonderful things God has already done. When you understand whatever happens is part of God's plan, your life will dramatically improve. You may even recognize the challenges you originally faced weren't as bad as you initially thought. Also by realizing God looks out for your best interest you can start feeling happier where you are in life. .

"Couldn't Have Done It Without You Lord. You Helped Me So Much!"

"We must be willing to let go of the life we have planned so as to have the life that is waiting for us."
English Novelist E..M. Forster

> **"Therefore I say to you, all things whatever things you ask when you pray, believe that you receive them, and you will have them."**
> **Mark 11:24 NKJV**

Be Careful What You Ask For!

Photo By Marty Ritzke

Sometimes I don't know if I should ask a question.
Someone might think I'm not smart. I might get the wrong answer, or not like it.
So Lord, please help me ask the right questions.

> "I have learned from personal experience that putting trust in God means there will be some unanswered questions. That was a hard lesson for me because I naturally want to understand everything... to know what's going on so I can feel like I'm in control."
> Christian Author Joyce Meyer

Be Careful What You Ask For!

As you know, challenges surround us. When they occur there are many opportunities to plow through them. Your reaction can make a difference in the outcome. You can do whatever you want to do. You can make strides towards achieving your goals and dreams, or you can simply let them go astray. You can let others get the best of you, or you can get the best out of yourself. Consequences depend upon your decisions. Sometimes your decision isn't to make one. That's okay. All of us at one time or another have experienced indecisiveness. Occasionally there is uncertainty. You aren't sure you're making the right decision. Believe me, you aren't the only one who's felt this way. I've had my share of indecision, where my decision isn't to make one.

Sometimes when faced with challenges you might want to turn to someone for guidance. Asking someone you respect for input and advice can make a difference in the outcome. The truth is, if you have questions about something don't be afraid or hesitate to ask someone. The worst thing that could happen is they might not have the answer, or make fun of you. Please know, asking questions won't make you look less intelligent. If anything, it makes you look smarter. Novelist Thomas Berger touched upon this fact when he mentioned: "The art and science of asking questions is the source of all knowledge." So true. To have a question and not ask it is simply limiting your ability to learn and improve yourself. You don't learn from always talking, texting or playing video games. My grandfather once said: "God gave you two ears, two eyes and one mouth. Therefore you should hear and see twice as much as you say." It's true you learn more by asking questions and listening.

With that in mind, think about what questions you want to ask beforehand. If you ask wrong questions, or ones that seem foolish, answers may be unpleasant. In 2 Timothy 2:23 KJV it says: "But foolish and unlearned questions avoid, knowing that they do gender strifes." The scripture reminds us that some questions can be misleading with undesirable results and might cause conflict, hostility, and bad feelings. So be careful not only what you ask for, but who you ask those questions to. Why not turn to God and ask Him what is best for you? In John 16:24 NKJV It says: "Until now, you have asked nothing in My name. Ask, and you will receive, that your joy may be full." In Matthew 7:7 KJV it says: "Ask, and it shall be given you; seek, and ye shall find; knock, and it shall be opened unto you." God wants you to turn to Him and ask questions. To spite your challenges, know God's answers are what is best for you. .

"It's True! God Always Answers My Questions!"

"Before you start some work, always ask yourself three questions - Why am I doing it, What the results might be and Will I be successful. Only when you think deeply you'll find satisfactory answers to these questions, go ahead."
Indian Philosopher Chanakya

Cast Your Cares Onto God!

Photo By Marty Ritzke

Lord, I don't like what people are doing. They keep picking on me.
I know they're not going to get the best of me, because I have You on my side!

"I really believe that all of us have a lot of darkness in our souls. Anger, rage,
fear, sadness. I don't think that's only reserved for people who have horrible
upbringings. I think it really exists and is part of the human condition. I think
in the course of your life you figure out ways to deal with that."
Actor Kevin Bacon

Cast Your Cares Onto God!

Life's challenges can cause people to act in ways that may provoke unpleasant even unavoidable problems later on. Most of us have experienced something like this, and that's okay. What is important is how you handle those unpleasant situations. No matter what you're going through, it's your decision how you will react to undesirable situations. You can blow things out of proportion and let situations bother you, or you can focus on finding ways to improve them. Like I've said before, you can let circumstances get the best of you or you can take action and do your best to get the most out of those situations. The latter is the more favorable choice. Your choice can impact the outcome you'll experience. With that in mind, it makes me think of a quote my father told me. "For every action there's a reaction, and the reaction sets the tone to the interaction."

Problems are unavoidable. At times they can be overwhelming. Sometimes it seems like there's no resolution. Ever notice when problems pull you down, you may stop looking at what you want in life? You might have had a dream you didn't pursue, or experienced something frightening or upsetting. You may feel you can't do something, or carry out a goal. Sometimes efforts go unnoticed and things don't turn out as planned. I like what author John Maxwell once said: "Problems are those things we see when we take our eyes off the goal." That is so true. What we focus on becomes our reality. It's easy to think: 'It's not working out. There's nothing I can do about _____.' Maybe you've experienced something like that. By thinking this way you're sending God a message you'd rather focus on the problems you're facing than on His solutions.

Difficult situations don't have to dominate your time and energy. Instead of getting frustrated or even annoyed at difficulties, why not use them to your advantage? Understand, these mishaps are God's way of teaching you important lessons. He wants these lessons to be learning tools to improve your life. You should realize, God has the solution to your problems even before they occur. With that in mind, why not let God take care of your concerns. The Bible talks about 'casting your cares and problems onto God.' It often mentions God takes pleasure when we cast our cares on Him. 1 Peter 5:7 NKJV states: "Cast all your anxiety on Him because He cares for you." A few things happen when we let God take care of our difficulties. Answers to questions come quicker, problems definitely get resolved with less effort, and your faith will get stronger. Once you are aware of this, experiencing life's challenges in stride gets easier. So why not cast your cares onto God. He will help you through them?

"You Mean If I Give It To God He'll Make It Better?"

"The greatest mistake we make is living in constant fear that we will make one."
Author John Maxwell

God Uses Setbacks As Stepping Stones!

Photo By Marty Ritzke

It sure is rough trying to get through life's disappointments.
Don't let them upset you. Instead, pull yourself up.
Use those setbacks as stepping stones and learn from those lessons.

"Life is a series of experiences, each one of which makes us bigger, even though sometimes
it is hard to realize this. For the world was built to develop character, and we must learn
that the setbacks and grieves which we endure help us in our marching onward."
Henry Ford

God Uses Setbacks As Stepping Stones!

All of us one time or another have experienced setbacks during our lives. Most likely you have gone through, or are experiencing some. It could be a relationship not working out, or a business plan that fell through. Maybe it's some bad news regarding a friend, or family member or even your health. Financial difficulties could be setting you back. Whatever it may be, you don't have to let setbacks pull you down. Instead, why not think of them as lessons, and learn from them?

Like I mentioned, God's lessons are stepping stones. Let's learn from them. God tests all of us throughout life with unpleasant situations. To pass God's test, understand when you get knocked down, don't stay down. Get back up again. In James 1:12 NKJV it says: "Blessed is the one who perseveres under trial because, having stood the test, that person will receive the crown of life that the Lord has promised to those who love him." So, if you want to see God's best, you must have faith. Know you can bounce back and make it through those tough times. Live by God's word. Like Psalm 37:23 NKJV says: "The steps of a good man are ordered by the Lord. And he delights in His way."

When setbacks try to throw you down, your thoughts shouldn't dictate your actions. The founder of Forbes Magazine, B. C. Forbes put it so well when he said: "History has demonstrated that the most notable winners usually encountered heartbreaking obstacles before they triumphed. They won because they refused to become discouraged by their defeats." It's easy to lose enthusiasm, get discouraged, or even be tempted to simply settle where you are. But don't. It gets easier to handle burdens that are weighing you down when you don't get discouraged. Why not shift your focus away from those troubles and turn to God knowing you can tell Him anything? Like it says in Matthew 11:28 NKJV: "Come to me, all you who labor and are heavily laden, and I will give you rest." So go ahead and tell God your concerns and trust that He can and will correct them.

God's Word emphasizes, even though life can be overwhelming, don't focus on setbacks, look up to Me. When turning to God, speak His word with belief. Understand His promises, and trust your life to His care. Realize God is in control and won't let you go through anything you can't handle. Every set back you experience is simply a set up for something better. So leave your problems to God. Allow Him to do only what He can do … preform miracles on you.

"You Mean Having Setbacks Is Really God Setting Us Up?"

"You have to know that every time adversity comes against you, it's a setup for a comeback!"
Pastor Joel Osteen

When You Fall Down, Get Right Up!

Photo By Marty Ritzke

Lord, thanks for not letting falling down get the best of me.
Instead You will help me get back up so I can keep on doing my best!

"Admit your failures quickly and humbly. The people already know
when you've erred, but they'll appreciate your right spirit."
Author John Maxwell

When You Fall Down, Get Right Up!

It's true, all of us one time or another fall down in life. You most likely have experienced something like that. I know I have, and it's okay. Life is full of annoying, difficult situations. Sometimes they seem far fetched, and can be hard to handle. Some may even seem unattainable. When that happens we should realize those situations are just a learning curve. When we fall down, we should get back up. Stick to your guns, hang in there and don't let difficult situations ruin your outlook on life. Zig Ziglar once said: "There is little you can learn from doing nothing." If you don't try, you'll never learn. Realize if you just persevere, regardless of the obstacles, those challenges will eventually work out in your favor. You may notice you are better off because of them.

You may experience situations that initially seem tough, but later on they're not so difficult. Someone once said: "What matters in life isn't how you start something, it's how you finish it." It doesn't matter where you are in your life's journey. What matters is that you finish. So, if you stumble in life, get back up and try again. A Japanese Proverb says: "Fall down seven times, get up eight times." What it's saying is don't give up. Bounce back and keep on trying. Understand, God wants His children to know when you fall, it's not the end. Difficulties are God's way of teaching you that some decisions and actions may not be what's best in the long run. To spite falling down, God's always there for you. Like the Psalm says in NKJV 37:24 "Though he may stumble, he will not fall, for the Lord upholds him with His hand."

There may be times where it seems like you can't escape the frustrations that keep prevailing. When that happens, remember, you can make one change that can make a difference in your life. That is, tap into your faith. Even though life will try to trip you, or even throw you down, please don't let it get the best of you. Don't let it stop your dreams or desires. Instead think of those falls as opportunities to get stronger and grow. People don't grow as much during easy times. However, they do grow more after going through tough times. The same holds true with you. God doesn't want you to experience adversity or go through difficult times if He didn't already have a plan for you. So keep the faith and turn to God. Let God know you trust Him. Let Him help you conquer your challenges. Follow His word believing He knows what's best for you. As you live by God's word and honor Him, realize He will turn those 'stumbling blocks' into 'stepping stones.'

"You'll Get Through It With God's Help!"

"I'm most proud of the blessings that God has bestowed upon me, in my life. He's given me the vision to truly see that you can fall down, but you can still get back up. Hopefully I'll learn from my mistakes and have the opportunity to strengthen and improve the next thing I do."
Actor Martin Lawrence

You Give Me The Strength To Keep Trying!

Photo By Marty Ritzke

Yeah, I don't like what's happening, but Lord, You're giving me the strength to keep trying! I know You're not going to let life's circumstances get the best of me.

"Every problem is a character-building opportunity, and the more difficult it is, the greater the potential for building spiritual muscle and moral fiber."
Pastor Rick Warren

You Give Me The Strength To Keep Trying!

Challenges are inevitable and shouldn't prevent you from achieving your goals and dreams. Somehow during those tough times you can find ways to get through them. You might have noticed, it took strength and determination to get what you wanted in life? I sure have. When challenges occur, tap into that inner strength God has given you. It'll help you get through those challenges. When you realize you don't have to struggle or control everything, stressful situations become easier to handle. You may already know God is in control. So why not turn your troubles over to Him? God wants you to realize though you're facing difficulties, He will use it for your own good. This is especially true when you believe nothing is too great for God to handle. God only wants what's best for you. Billy Graham put it so well when he once said: "God is more interested in your future and your relationships than you are."

Somehow, throughout your troubles, whether big or small, God is there for you. He gives you the necessary strength to get through whatever you're experiencing. So when you are up against some problems call on the Lord. He hears your prayers. In Psalm 86:7 WEB it says: "In the day of my trouble I will call on you, for you will answer me." God will answer your prayers. Sometimes it may not seem like it, especially when prayers aren't answered right away. Instead of getting annoyed, frustrated, or saddened, understand, God heard you the first time you prayed. He will answer prayers when He feels the time is right. Be patient and confident, knowing God's timing is what is best for all.

Maybe you've heard the analogy that life's like a story in a novel. Events that occur are like chapters in a book. God plans your life accordingly, and has already written the final chapter in your life's story. As you go through life you may not even be aware of that. By realizing you are in God's hands, it gets easier to let go of those burdens, and simply allow Him to guide you through life. Like it says in James 1:12 WEB: "Blessed is the man who endures temptation, for when he has been approved, he will receive the crown of life, which the Lord promised to those who love Him." Realize, in the midst of turmoil rests knowledge. By understanding you are exactly where you should be, it becomes easier to tap into your inner strength and conquer life's challenges in stride. .

"So True! God Is There For Us!"

"We can be tired, weary and emotionally distraught, but after spending time alone with God, we find that He injects into our bodies energy, power and strength."
Pastor Charles Stanley

God Will Renew Your Strength!

Photo By Marty Ritzke

God's given me certain gifts and talents so I can be the best I can possibly be.
He's given me the necessary strength to venture out and do just that.

God Will Renew Your Strength!

You may have noticed in the midst of turmoil rests knowledge, especially when you tap into faith. It sure is comforting knowing insight is obtainable and within reach. Often those who carefully reach for it can grasp the lessons to be learned. Sometimes effort seems strenuous, achievements questionable, goals and dreams seem far fetched. But among these challenges, lies clarity to the mental confusion. To spite what you're experiencing, when you exercise caution, God will reward you with favor and blessings. So be aware of that as you carefully and cheerfully experience each day to its fullest.

During times of trouble, when turmoil prevails, try to be more like an eagle. In Deuteronomy 32:11 WEB it says: "As an eagle that stirs up her nest, that flutters over her young, he spread abroad his wings, he took them, he bore them on his feathers." Our Father does that in our lives. With God's help you can soar like an eagle. Also in Jeremiah 48:40 NKJV it says: "For thus says the Lord: 'Behold, one shall fly like an eagle, And spread his wings over Moab.'" Eagles truly are powerful. Their excellent eyesight allows them to see what they want way in advance. They can fly to an altitude near 10,000 feet at speeds around 30 to 35 mph while maintaining flight without flapping their wings. They soar on thermal conviction and rising air currents.

Ever notice eagles don't hang around those that threaten them? Instead, when troubles and threats prevail the eagle simply takes flight and soars higher, where other birds won't go. God created the eagle and gave it knowledge, insight and capability to fly high, above the rest. He has also done that for all of His children. He will look after you and pick you up in times of trouble. He'll also guide you to safety when needed. Realize your life is in God's hands. He renews your strength when needed.

God wants you to fly like the eagles and soar to higher places than you ever imagined. In order to do that, believe in your abilities, and trust God, knowing He knows what's best for you. He will lead you in the right direction, above limitations and mockery people put on you. If necessary He'll create conditions like air currents to help you soar on His thermal conviction towards the destiny He designed for you. The eagle's talons grasp what they want and don't let go of it until they are ready to. You can do the same with your dreams and goals. God gives each of us the ability to achieve those aspirations. He wants you to succeed. So let's not be like not like the turkeys, pigs and other critters that have limitations in their beliefs about what they can do. Let's be more like the mystical eagle, Fly above the rest and allow God to renew your strength so you can live life to its fullest. I think you'll like the outcome. .

"I'm Gonna Go Places Thanks To God!"

"God sent me on earth. He sent me to do something, and nobody can stop me. If God wants to stop me, then I stop. Man never can."
Songwriter Bob Marley

In Summary:

Inevitably life is full of challenges you have to get through. If you're not sure what to do next, simply be still and don't let your thoughts, electronic gadgets or any other distractions take you away from this quiet time. When challenges occur, try to be still and worship God. Allow Him to quiet your inner voice. Like it says in Psalms 46:10 WEB: "Be still and know that I am God." Quiet moments with God can help reduce a lot of stress in life. They also shift thoughts away from life's frustrations to more calming and pleasant thoughts. When you're still, you can comfortably rest, knowing God is in control. You'll notice by being still it becomes easier shifting thoughts from yourself to God and His interests. So, why not be still, and know that He is God. Worship Him and know He loves and cares for you.

Be open-minded in how you react to negative circumstances. Try not to let situations get the best of you. Instead, simply let them go, and allow God to take care of them. By channeling your energy more productively it becomes easier to get the best out of life, before it gets the best out of you. You'll also notice when you follow God's word and do what He is calling you to do, it will not only bring you joy, God will give you abundant blessings. So be kind and offer love to others, Help those in need, for we may one day need that ourselves. Also, be grateful for the gifts and blessings God has and will continue giving you. Tap into these gifts with vim and vigor knowing God gave them for a reason.

Sometimes you need to shift thoughts away from yourself and life's challenges and focus more on God's interests and lessons. One way to minimize stress and find more happiness is to pray. So pray to God and ask Him to help you shut off the noise around you and not be distracted. Allow God to quiet your inner voice. Let Him to guide you towards your dreams and aspirations. It says in Psalm 144:15 NKJV: "Happy are the people whose God is the Lord." It also says in 1 Thessalonians 5:18 NKJV: "Rejoice always, pray continually, give thanks in all circumstances, for this is God's will for you..."

If you've been blessed and things are going great, that's fantastic. Even if you're content with life, allow yourself time with God through prayer and give thanks. Understand your prayers are being heard, and answered, when the time is right. Realize this quiet time spent with God is a magnificent de-stressor and is rather beneficial to one's overall health. In Philippians 1:6 NIV it states: "Be confident of this very thing, that God who has begun a good work in you will complete it." God wants all of us to know that. In Psalm 32:8 NKJV it shows how God will guide us through life. "I will instruct you and teach you in the way you should go; I will council you with my loving eye on you."

One thing is for certain, anytime is better than no time to spend with God. Remember to be still and pray, knowing He is always on your side. Understand at all times He is God. He loves and cares for you and will see you through your challenges. Think of it like He is our captain, the driver who is in control, and we are simply His passengers. Let's see where He will take us. In the interim we might as well have fun on this ride in life. So what's the next step? Well, fasten your seatbelt cause God's going to take you for a ride through life. Let's make this ride more fun and enjoy spending more time with God.

God Wants You to Fasten Your Seatbelt.

There are so many roads to go down in life. Which one is best for you? This is what you need to figure out. No doubt you will you find that out as you go through life's trials and tribulations. When going through tough times try keeping a good attitude. That's what God wants you to do. Even though life's struggles are inevitable, there's always a way of finding some balance. There is so much to learn through your travels in life. Many of the roads are hilly. Some are quite steep. You'll also find some roads are flat, mundane and quite predictable. Life is a lot like this.

Sometimes the roads you go down provide a direct path to your destination. Other times they simply take you out of the way from achieving your goals. There are times you may need a map to help you get back on track. Maps are merely beneficial guidelines that can simplify your life and educate you when needed. God wants you to take the time to read and study them knowing they can assist you during your needs. The Bible is similar. Think of it as life's map. Learn the Words of God and live by them. You'll find in life, each road you travel down has a lesson to be learned.

You may have to travel down many roads in life before finding what comes naturally. Throughout life's travels, your destiny becomes more obvious. God knows there are many ditches that need to be avoided, chuck holes to stay away from and detours to be expected. He wants you to know although they're not always pleasant, one way roads, speed bumps and road closed signs are all part of His plan. Also, construction is evident. The fact is, God wants you to understand those repercussions we experience through life's travels are well worth the hassles they bring to us.

When experiencing the numerous intersections and turns, you must yield to oncoming traffic. Accidents usually happen when you don't pay attention to those details. There's a large number of people racing around and in such a hurry to get things done. By simply accelerating through life, it becomes evident you are diverting your attention. In essence, you're allowing outcomes to sharply turn, even steal your focus from your dreams. In doing so, you often fall victim, and crash into those undesirable circumstances. Many times it may not be intentional, but the consequences of your actions can often be unpleasant.

God wants you to know that a dream fueled by purpose will accelerate desirable results. Dreams are favorable and more likely to happen when you slam the brakes to negativity, self sabotage, doubt, fear, frustration, hostility, anger, and other detrimental thoughts and actions. God is telling you those negative traits are just warning signs. There may be problems down the road if you keep on that path. On your life's destiny there will be signs and caution signals that you need pay attention to and abide by. It's important to observe and learn from life's many lessons.

Respectfully follow the path God has planned for you. Please know when you cruise down life's path, you need to be careful, especially since others aren't always doing the same. By doing this, your travels along life's many roads will be more like a joy ride. There is a light at the end of the tunnel. To spite the hard rough roads you may be going down, you have so much to be grateful for. You must follow the path God's designed for you. God wants you to keep driving forward in life knowing you have to experience some bad so you can appreciate the good. Remember to look ahead, for the windshield is much larger that the rear view mirror. Look down the road in life and know, your future has so much to offer. God has in store many blessings for you!

...~... So why not fasten your seat belt and enjoy the ride. ...~...

Recommended Books To Read:

The Holy Bible New King James Version, NKJV
The Holy Bible New International Version, NIV
The New Living Testament ~ Tyndale House Publishers
The Messenger The New Testament Psalms and Proverbs ~ Eugine H. Peterson NAVPRESS
Colorado Springs CO 1995
Possibility Thinkers Bible ~ Robert H. Schuller Thomas Nelson Inc. Nashville, Cadmen New York 1984

Other Spiritual and Scripture Oriented Books

Daily Inspiration For The Purpose Driven Life ~ By Rick Warren, Zondervan Corporation, Grand Rapids, MI. 2004

365 Positive Thoughts Hope for Today And Tomorrow ~ The Reverend Dr. Robert H. Schuller, Garden Grove, CA Crystal Cathedral Ministries, 1998

It's Your Time ~ Joel Osteen, Free Press, 2009

Become A Better You 7 Keys to Improving Your Life ~ Joel Osteen, Free Press, 2007

Daily Readings from Become A Better You 90 Devotions for Improving Your Life ~ Joel Osteen Free Press, 2008

Your Best Life Now 7 Steps to Living At Your Full Potential ~ Joel Osteen, Time Warner Book Group, 2004

The Power Of I AM ~ Joel Osteen, Faith Words Machete Book Group, 2015

There's A Spiritual Solution To Every Problem ~ Wayne Dyer, Harper Collins Publishers, 2001

Jesus Calling Enjoying Peace In His Presence. ~ Sarah YoungThomas Nelson Inc, 2004

"The best advice I ever got was that knowledge is power and to keep reading."
Author David Bailey

"A truly good book teaches me better than to read it. I must soon lay it down, and commence living on its hint. What I began by reading, I must finish by acting."
Author Henry David Thoreau

Other Awesome Books To Read:

Don't Sweat The Small Stuff. . . And It's All Small Stuff ~ Richard Carlson, Ph.D., Hyperion, New York, NY, 1997

The Big Book of Small Stuff ... 100 of The Best Inspirations From DON'T SWEAT THE SMALL STUFF Richard Carlson, Ph.D.,Hyperion, New York, NY, 2007

Success Through A Positive Mental Attitude ~ Napoleon Hill and W.Clement Stone, Pocket Books, Simon & Schuster Inc, 1977

Something to Smile About ~ Zig Ziglar, Thomas Nelson Publishers, Nashville TN, 1997

Unlimited Power ~ Anthony Robbins, Ballantine Books, New York NY, 1986

Awaken The Giant Within ~ Anthony Robbins, Simon & Schuster Inc., 1991

Today Matters ~ John C. Maxwell, Time Warner Book Group, 2004

Success . . . One Day At A Time ~ John C. Maxwell, J. Countryman, Nashville TN, 2000

Love, Medicine & Miracles ~ Bernie S. Siegel M.D., Harper Row Publishers Inc. New York, NY, 1986

The Power Is Within You ~ Louise L. Hay, Hay House Inc, 1991

The Success Principles ~ Jack Canfield, Harper Resource Book, New York, NY, 2005

Feel free to contact me, as I would love to hear from you.
For ordering and information concerning other products please contact me at:
e-mail: inspirationsjust4U@gmail.com

I want to wish you a life full of happiness and God's Blessings.

Cut Along Dotted Line

- -

Product Order Form

Full Name:

First Name | Last Name

Mailing Address:

Street Address | City

State / Province | Zip Code | Country

Phone Number:

Area Code | Phone Number

E-Mail:

Product Ordered:

Books

Greeting Cards

Photos from Books or Website

Additional Requests:

Method Of Payment: Master Card ☐   Visa ☐   Pay-Pal ☐   Check / Money Order ☐

Credit Card Number | Security Code

I Want To Thank You For Your Order.   *May God Continue To Bless You. . .*

CPSIA information can be obtained
at www.ICGtesting.com
Printed in the USA
BVHW021458250319
543613BV00036B/2901/P